SPIRAL SLIDE RULE.

EQUIVALENT TO

A STRAIGHT SLIDE RULE 83 FEET 4 INCHES LONG,
OR, A CIRCULAR RULE 13 FEET 3 INCHES
IN DIAMETER.

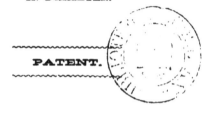

PATENT.

GEORGE FULLER, M. INST. C.E.,
PROFESSOR OF ENGINEERING IN THE QUEEN'S UNIVERSITY, IRELAND.

10 .

LONDON:

E. & F. N. SPON, 46, CHARING CROSS.
NEW YORK: 446, BROOME STREET.
1878.

SPIRAL SLIDE RULE.

THE method of performing by mechanical means
the work of addition and subtraction required
when multiplying and dividing numbers by
means of logarithms, originated with Gunter
about the year 1606. He constructed a linear
scale which was composed of two equal parts,
and each half divided into parts proportional to
the logarithms of numbers from 10 to 100. With
this scale he used a pair of compasses for making
the additions and subtractions.

About the year 1630, Oughtred invented the
two similar logarithmic scales sliding in contact, which are at present in use; and he is
stated to have used both straight and concentric
circular scales. The advantage of this arrangement is, that the result is obtained by one
motion of the sliding scale; and not only are
multiplication and division thus worked, but
questions in proportion, or the combination of
the two, are solved by a single movement of the
slide.

The simplicity of this method of calculating
with figures is so great, that it seems strange it

has not been more used; but the following considerations will, it is believed, account for this :—

In testing the relative advantages of different methods of making arithmetical calculations, the mental effort required, the time occupied, and the truth of the result have all to be taken into account. Now, in judging the ordinary slide rule by these points, it will be found that the facilities it offers are more apparent than real.

It is easy, with a little practice, to place one of the lines of the slide either opposite to a division of the rule or in a required position between two divisions, if these are not very close together. When the space, however, between two consecutive marks is very small, then great difficulty arises, from the strain upon the eyesight and the minute motion of the slide.

For example, in the ordinary slide rule with the scale $5\frac{1}{2}$ inches long, the breadth of the division from 99 to 100 is about $\frac{1}{40}$ of an inch. Therefore to mark such a number as 996, this space must be mentally divided into ten equal parts, each part consequently being $\frac{1}{400}$ of an inch, a magnitude quite inappreciable without a magnifying glass. The effort and time for the above is, however, slight, compared to that required when a point on one scale between two divisions has to be placed or read as agreeing with a point on the other, also between two divisions. For in this case (which is the most common, owing to the number of divisions on the ordinary slide rule necessarily being few) the division on one scale has to be mentally divided, and the particular point required fixed in the mind by its distance from the nearest division. Then the division on the other scale has to be mentally divided, and that part of it read which agrees with the point on the first scale previously fixed in the mind. Thus, for example, suppose it is required to place 554 on one scale to agree with 643 on the other. There are marks at 55 and 56 on one scale, and at 64 and 65 on the other; but the $\frac{4}{10}$ part of the distance between 55 and 56 has to be made to coincide with the $\frac{3}{10}$ part of that between 64 and 65 : the difficulty not being to divide either of these distances into ten parts, if they are not very small, but to combine the two operations together.

If at the same time the spaces between the marks are very small, the difficulty is greatly increased by the strain upon the eyesight.

With regard to the truth of the result, Mr. Heather, in his 'Treatise on Mathematical Instruments,' writes in relation to the foot slide rule : "The solution in fact may be considered as obtained to within a two-hundredth part of the whole." Now this approximation, though close considering the length of scale of the instrument, and sufficient for some, is not near enough for very many of the calculations required by engineers and architects.

From the above it appears that a slide rule to

be thoroughly efficient, so that calculations may be made by it with ease and rapidity, and practically correct results obtained, the length of the logarithmic scale should be such that the space between any two consecutive numbers is large enough to be easily distinguished by the unaided eye; that the scale should be read by indices, and not as in the present rules; and that the number of divisions should be so great and distinctly marked, that the result to be obtained may be easily read and practically correct.

This combination, it is believed, is attained in the spiral slide rule.

The rule consists of a cylinder (d) that can be moved up and down upon, and turned round, an axis (f), which is held by a handle (e). Upon this cylinder is wound in a spiral a single logarithmic scale. Fixed to the handle is an index (b). Two other indices (c) and (a), whose distance apart is the axial length of the complete spiral, are fixed to the cylinder (g). This cylinder slides in (f) like a telescope tube, and thus enables the operator to place these indices in any required position relative to (d). Two stops (o) and (p) are so fixed that when they are brought in contact, the index (b) points to the commencement of the scale. (n) and (m) are two scales, the one on the piece carrying the movable indices, the other on the cylinder (d).

It will at once be seen that by this arrangement the length of the logarithmic scale can be

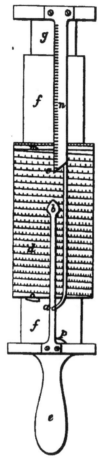

Scale, 3 inches to a foot.

made very great, whilst keeping the instrument
of a convenient size for use. It requires only
one logarithmic scale, so that every inch of the
spiral scale is equivalent to two of the ordinary
straight rule.

To fulfil with great exactness all the necessary
conditions, the scale is made 500 inches, or 41 feet
8 inches, long—equivalent therefore to a straight
rule 83 feet 4 inches long, and to a circular rule
13 feet 3 inches in diameter. This allows of
results being obtained to one ten thousandth part
of the whole, at the same time requiring no space
less than $\frac{1}{10}$ of an inch, between any two consecutive numbers of four figures. The length of scale
in the common rule only permits of the *first* figure
of a number being printed; in this rule, the first
three figures are printed throughout the scale.
With this rule, to produce an error of one part in
200, there must be, either in setting or reading,
an error of *one and one-tenth* inches. It will also be
seen that both for setting and reading, indices are
applied to the scale; so that these operations are
performed with the greatest mental ease.

It may be remarked that the slide rule pos-
sesses an advantage over a table of logarithms, in
addition to that of performing mechanically the
requisite additions and subtractions, in that the
approximation is uniform throughout the scale,
and not nearer in one part than in another, as in
the tables.

It must be remembered that all the calculations

founded on measurements of length, weight, and
time, can only be approximative, as the data for
them are so. Except therefore with the most re-
fined measurements, it is a waste of time to carry
results beyond the ten thousandth part of the
whole.

RULES.

In using the slide rule, the handle should be
held in the left hand, the movable cylinder and
indices being worked by the right, which holds
the pen or pencil.

Division of the Scale.—Though this scale is large
enough to admit of being read to four or even
five figures, space does not allow of its being
figured to more than three. Each of the primary
divisions, as far as 650, is divided into ten parts,
and from thence to 1000 into five parts; so that
all numbers of four figures have either a mark
upon the scale, or are midway between two
marks. Thus 4786 is shown by a mark; also
8432; but 8431 is not shown by a mark, but
is midway between 8430 and 8432. In a large
part of the scale the space between these secondary divisions is large enough to be easily
divided into parts by the eye. Thus many
numbers of five figures are easily shown; for
example, 26854. There are the first three figures
at 268, then 5 is at the fifth secondary division,
and the 4 must be estimated by the eye as $\frac{4}{10}$ of
the space between 2685 and 2686. It must be noted

that the same figures do not always mea
same amount.   Thus to represent 268540, ?
2685·4, 268·54, 26·854, 2·6854, ·26854, ·0?
·0026854, &c., the same point on the scale i?

MULTIPLICATION.

Rule.—Bring 100 to the fixed index, and
the movable index to the multiplicand.
move the cylinder so that the multiplier is
fixed index.   The quotient is read off at
the movable indices.

To ascertain the Value of the Quotient.—Mo
quently this may be determined by inspectio:
following rules will, however, give it in all ca

Consider a number like—

18763	as one of 5 figures	
1876·3	„	4 „
187·63	„	3 „
18·763	„	2 „
1·8763	„	1 „
·18763	„	0 „
·018763	„	−1 „
·0018763	„	−2 „
·000187	„	−3 „

Then the number of figures in the quot
the algebraic sum of the number of figures
multiplier and multiplicand, if it is *not* rea(
the same index as the multiplicand.   It is (
than that sum if read upon the same index.

Examples.—12 × ·142 = 1·704.   The s?

figures is two, and the answer is read from the same index as the multiplicand, so that the quotient has one figure.

$64 \times \cdot24 = 15\cdot36$. The sum of figures is two, but the answer is read at a different index to the multiplicand, and therefore the quotient has two figures.

$12 \times \cdot00142 = \cdot01704$. The sum of the figure is 0, but the answer is read at the same index with the multiplicand, and therefore the quotient has one less, or minus one.

$64 \times \cdot0024 = \cdot1536$. The sum of the figures is 0, and the answer is read at a different index to the multiplicand, and therefore the quotient has 0 figures.

$48\cdot42 \times 64\cdot34 = 3115\cdot3$. The sum of the figures is 4, and the answer is read at a different index to the multiplicand, and therefore the quotient has four figures.

DIVISION.

Rule.—Place *divisor* to fixed index, and the upper or lower movable index to the dividend, according as the first figure in the divisor is greater or less than the first figure in the dividend. Then move the cylinder so that the fixed index is at 100, and read the quotient at one of the movable indices.

The number of figures in the quotient is the algebraic *difference* between the number of figures in the dividend and divisor, if it is *not* read upon the same index as the dividend. It is one *more* than that difference if read upon the same index.

Examples.—1468 ÷ 63 = 23·3, as the difference is 2, and the quotient is *not* read upon the same index as the dividend.

1468 ÷ 125 = 11·7, as the difference is 1, and the quotient *is* read upon the same index as the dividend, and therefore has *two* figures.

·1468 ÷ 63 = ·00233, as the difference is − 2, and the quotient is *not* read upon the same index as the dividend, and therefore has − 2 figures.

1468 ÷ ·00125 = 1174000, as the difference is 4 − (− 2) = 4 + 2 = 6, and the quotient *is* read upon the same index as the dividend, and therefore has *seven* figures.

MULTIPLICATION AND DIVISION.

Rule.—Move the cylinder so as to place the denominator to the fixed index. Then place movable index to one of the numerators. Then move the cylinder so that the fixed index points to the other numerator, and read the quotient at one of movable indices.

The number of figures in the quotient is the algebraic difference between the sum of the number of figures in the numerator and in the denominator, if it is read upon the *same* index as a factor of the numerator. It is *one more* than that difference if read upon the other index.

Example. $\dfrac{4854 \times 32·6}{536} = 295·22$, as the difference is $4 + 2 - 3 = 3$, and the quotient is read at the same index as either 4854 or 32·6 is placed.

$$\frac{·0764 \times ·032}{14·63} = ·000167,$$ as the difference is

$(-1) + (-1) - 2 = -4$, and the quotient is not read upon the index, that either ·0764 or ·032 is placed, and therefore *the number* of figures is -3.

To multiply three numbers together when one of them is a constant in frequent use.

Rule.—Find the *reciprocal* of the constant by division, and use it as the divisor in the preceding rule.

RATIO.

When either of the movable indices is at one number and the fixed index at another, and the cylinder is turned into any other position, though the numbers at the indices will be different, their ratio will remain constant.

Example.—To convert francs and centimes into sterling money, supposing exchange 25f. 45c. for 1*l.* The ratio between centimes and pence is 2545 to 240. Place the cylinder so that the fixed index is at 2545, and make one of the movable indices point to 240. Then on moving the cylinder to read off different numbers of centimes at the fixed index, the corresponding value in pence will be read at the movable index.

Wages Table.—To find the wages for different times at 35*s.* per week of 57 hours. Place the

cylinder so that the fixed index is at 57, and make one of the movable indices point to 420, the number of pence in 85s. Then on moving the cylinder to read off different numbers of hours at the fixed index, the corresponding wages in pence will be read at the movable index.

PROPORTION.

To find a third proportion to two numbers—
$a : b :: b : c$

$c = \dfrac{b \times b}{a}$. Proceed according to rule for multiplication and division.

To find a fourth proportion to three numbers—
$a : b :: c : d$

$d = \dfrac{b \times c}{a}$. Proceed according to rule for multiplication and division.

POWERS AND ROOTS.

To obtain the square, cube, and fourth power of a number. The quickest way with this rule is by direct multiplication.

For higher powers and roots. Place the upper movable index (c) to the number, and read the scales (n and m). These together give the *mantissa* of the logarithm of the number. To this the *index* has to be added. The index of the logarithm of a number greater than unity is *one less* than the number of figures in the integral part of that number. Thus the index of 5432 is 3, of 543·2 is 2, of 54·32 is 1, and of 5·432 is 0.

Multiply or divide the resulting number by the power or root, as shown above. Then place the cylinder so that it reads on the scales (n and m) the decimal part of the quotient. The power or root is then at the index (c). In the result the number of figures before the decimal point is *one more* than the number in the integral part of the above quotient.

The scale (n) is read from the *lowest line* of the top spiral and (m) from the vertical edge of the scale (n).

Examples.—5^{13}, on placing (c) to 500, scale (n) reads ·68 and scale (m) ·01897, which gives the logarithm of 5 — ·69897, the index being 0. Then ·69897 × 13 = 9·08661. Now placing the cylinder so that it reads ·08661 on scales (n and m) the index (c) reads 12207, and the required power is 1220700000, having 10 figures, as the integral part of the above quotient is 9.

$\sqrt[5]{741}$ on placing (c) to 741, scale (n) reads ·86 and scale (m) ·00982 which gives the logarithm of 741 — 2·86982, the index being 2. Then 2·86982 ÷ 5 = ·57396. Now placing the cylinder so that it reads ·57396 on scales (n and m) the index (c) reads 37495, and the required root is 3·7495, having one figure before the decimal point, as the integral part of the above quotient is 0.

POWERS OF DECIMAL FRACTIONS.

To avoid the use of negative indices, which often lead to erroneous results unless they are frequently used, the following method may be adopted :—

Write them as vulgar fractions, the numerator being expressed in units and decimals, and raise the numerator and denominator to the required power, the former by the method given above; the latter can be written down at once.

$$\text{Thus } \cdot47^3 = \left(\frac{4 \cdot 7}{10}\right)^3 \qquad \cdot047^3 = \left(\frac{4 \cdot 7}{100}\right)^3$$

Roots of Decimal Fractions.

Write them as vulgar fractions, and multiply numerator and denominator by ten or a power of ten, so that the denominator may have a complete root. Then take the required root of the numerator by the method given above, and of the denominator by inspection :

$$\text{Thus } \sqrt{\cdot4} = \sqrt{\frac{4}{10}} = \sqrt{\frac{40}{10^2}} = \frac{\sqrt{40}}{10}$$

$$\sqrt[3]{\cdot04} = \sqrt[3]{\frac{4}{10^2}} = \sqrt[3]{\frac{40}{10^3}} = \frac{\sqrt[3]{40}}{10}$$

$$\sqrt[3]{\cdot586} = \sqrt[3]{\frac{586}{10^3}} = \sqrt[3]{\frac{58600}{10^5}} = \frac{\sqrt[3]{58600}}{10}$$

$$\sqrt[3]{\cdot00065} = \sqrt[3]{\frac{65}{10^5}} = \sqrt[3]{\frac{650}{10^6}} = \frac{\sqrt[3]{650}}{10^2}$$

$$(\cdot0434)^{\frac{3}{5}} = \left(\frac{434}{10^4}\right)^{\frac{3}{5}} = \left(\frac{43400}{10^6}\right)^{\frac{3}{5}} = \frac{(43400)^{\frac{3}{5}}}{10^5}$$

SIMPLE INTEREST.

Let P be the Principal in pounds and parts of
    a pound;
    n the number of years and parts of a year
      for which interest is taken;
    r the interest of one pound for one year;
    M the amount.
    $M = P + P\,n\,r.$

Also P is the present value of M, due at the end
of the time n.

$$P = \frac{M}{1 + n\,r}.$$

In practice the *discount* is the interest of the
sum of money paid before it is due;

$$\text{or } D = M\,n\,r.$$

COMPOUND INTEREST.

Let P be the Principal in pounds and parts of
    a pound;
    n number of years for which interest is
      taken;
    r the interest of one pound for one year;
    M the amount.

Interest due once a year.

$$M = P(1 + r)^n \qquad n = \frac{\log. M - \log. P}{\log. (1 + r)}$$

Let interest be due q times a year and $\dfrac{r}{q}$ the

interest of one pound for $\dfrac{1}{q}$ part of a year,

$$M = P\left(1 + \frac{r}{q}\right)^{q\,n}.$$

VALUE OF r.

Per Cent.		Per Cent.		Per Cent.		Per Cent.		Per Cent.	
$\frac{1}{32}$	·000625	$\frac{3}{16}$	·00375	$\frac{11}{32}$	·006875	1	·01	6	·0(
$\frac{1}{16}$	·00125	$\frac{7}{32}$	·004375	$\frac{3}{8}$	·0075	2	·02	7	·0
$\frac{3}{32}$	·001875	$\frac{1}{4}$	·005	$\frac{13}{32}$	·008125	3	·03	8	·0
$\frac{1}{8}$	·0025	$\frac{9}{32}$	·005625	$\frac{7}{16}$	·00875	4	·04	9	·(
$\frac{5}{32}$	·003125	$\frac{5}{16}$	·00625	$\frac{15}{32}$	·009375	5	·05	10	·

The tables printed on the rule have been mad
and selected as those considered most usefu
Owing to our want of a decimal system, it h
been deemed most important to have a serie
of tables which give for our measures of weigh
length, time, &c., the equivalent decimal fracti
of the larger for successive numbers of tl
smaller unit. This enables results to be obtaine
without the necessity of reduction. Thus to fir
the area of a rectangle whose sides are 24′ 6
and 43′ 5½″. The table gives by inspect
·5208 and ·4583 opposite 6½″ and 5½″ respe
tively, so that the area is obtained by multiplyi
24·521 by 43·458. The result, as shown by t
rule, is 1065·6. If the parts of a square f
are required in twelfths, the table shows th
·6 of a foot is equivalent to 7¼ twelfths, and tl
result reads 1065 − 7¼.

LONDON: PRINTED BY WILLIAM CLOWES AND SONS, STAMFORD STREE
AND CHARING CROSS.

Lightning Source UK Ltd.
Milton Keynes UK
UKHW020759121222
413794UK00007B/553

9 781015 641990

The Second Trial and Capital Conviction of
Daniel Dawson, for Poisoning Horses at
Newmarket in 1809, Before Mr. Justice
Heath at Cambridge On Wednesday the 22D
of July, 1812

THE

SECOND TRIAL

OF

DANIEL DAWSON,

FOR

Poisoning Horses;

Price, Two Shillings.

THE

SECOND TRIAL

AND

CAPITAL CONVICTION

OF

DANIEL DAWSON,

For Poisoning Horses,

AT NEWMARKET, IN 1809,

Before Mr. JUSTICE HEATH, at Cambridge,

On WEDNESDAY, the 22d of July, 1812,

TAKEN IN COURT,

BY GEO. KENT.

LONDON:

Printed by W. GLINDON, Rupert Street, Haymarket;

TO BE HAD OF THE AUTHOR, 8, DUFOUR'S-PLACE, GOLDEN-SQUARE;
R. ROGERS, NEWMARKET, OF WHOM THE COUNTRY TRADE
CAN BE SUPPLIED; HUGHES, LUDGATE-HILL;
AND MASON, NORTH AUDLEY-STREET;

1812.

L. Eng. B 75 e. Poisoning. 1

TRIAL

OF

DANIEL DAWSON.

—

THE Court was opened at seven o'clock in the morning, and every avenue was thronged, so as frequently to impede business. Dawson was brought into the Dock soon after; he looked extremely well, and saluted many of his friends who had assembled in Court, with the utmost cheerfulness. Lord Stawell, Mr. Northey, and many other sporting gentlemen took their stations on the bench with the Judge.

———

DANIEL DAWSON, of Burwell, in the County of Cambridge, was indicted for feloniously, wilfully, and maliciously infusing white arsenic into a watering trough at Newmarket, on the 10th of July 1809, and thereby poisoning a mare, value £20 the property of Mr. Adams, of Royston. There were three other counts in the indictment, varying the form.

The prisoner was arraigned on a second indictment charging him with poisoning a blood mare, value £20 the property of Mr. Northey, on the 10th of July also.

Another indictment charged him with poisoning a horse, value £1000 the property of Sir F. Standish, at Newmarket, in 1811, by unlawfully, wilfully, and maliciously procuring one Cecil Bishop, by promise of money and division of bets, to infuse poison into the troughs occupied by Mr. R. Prince.

The fourth and last indictment on which the prisoner was arraigned, was for poisoning Periouette, the property of Lord Foley, in 1811.

The two last bills of indictment were found at Cambridge, during the assizes, charging Dawson with having been an accessary before the fact of poisoning, he having been indicted at a former assize as principal in the poisoning act, and acquitted on an objection taken by Mr. King, as will be seen by reference to the pamphlet published on that occasion.

The prisoner pleaded not guilty to the several indictments, and on being asked in the usual way, if he had any objection to any of the Jury, he replied,— " No, my lord, the gentlemen are all strangers to me, and I can have no objection to any of them."

The following twelve Jurymen were then sworn:

ROBERT FULLER,	CARTER TYSON,
THOMAS WEBB,	JAMES FULLER,
JAMES COLLING,	JAMES NORMAN,
WM. FARLEY,	GEORGE BARNES,
RICHARD FEW,	JOHN SCOTT,
THO. PORTER,	J. BEACHEY,

The Counsel for the Prosecution, were Serjeant SELLON, and Messrs. BEST and STORK, and the Solicitors were Messrs. HOOPER and BROUGHTON, gentlemen of the first respectability, residing in Great Marlborough-Street. Mr. KING defended the prisoner wiih Mr. HARMER, an eminent Old Bailey Solicitor.

The prisoner was tried on the indictment, charging him with poisoning Mr. Adams's mare.

Mr. STORK opened the case, and Serjeant SELLON addressed the Jury as follows ;—

Gentlemen,

The offence with which the prisoner stands charged is recognised by an act of parliament, called the *black act*, which provides against unlawfully and maliciously destroying cattle. I shall not occupy your time by entering on the law of the case, because the learned judge, whose peculiar province it is to enlighten you on that subject, will promulgate it with his accustomed wisdom. I shall content myself with a detail of facts attending the case, to which I must intreat your particular attention. One general observation however arises; I shall prove distinctly that the mare, the subject of this indictment, was poisoned by infusing arsenic into the troughs, and the next point for your consideration, is, whether the prisoner at the bar so infused the poison into the water. If you are of that opinion, I submit to the learned judge, that malice against the owner was implied, and the case will be complete. Gentlemen, you must know that Newmarket is a place of turf amusement, where several meetings are held in a year, and the horses are in the care of training grooms, who reside there to prepare them for running. There are in truth seven meetings in the year, the *Craven*, the *first spring*, the *July*, and others in the autumn,

It was in the July meeting that this offence was committed. Amongst the training grooms to whom I have alluded, is a Mr. Stevens, in whose care the horse, the subject of this indictment, was intrusted, as well as others of different value, amongst which was a horse named *Woodwellhead,* the property of General Grosvenor. The traing grooms have their respective troughs, and it was generally known that an alarm had been raised in consequence of horses having been poisoned, and particular persons were suspected. These troughs are kept covered, but not so closely as to prevent the introduction of a straw or a syringe. Your attention will be particularly directed to Monday, the 10th of July, on which day the meeting commenced, and also on Saturday the 8th, to which days the evidence I am about to call, will particularly apply. Amongst the horses watered on the Monday morning, was *Woodwellhead,* a great favourite, two mares of Mr Northey's, one of Sir C. Bunburys, and Mr. Adams's hackney. After returning from water, the horses heads were tied up as usual, for dressing, and on giving them corn the animals refused it. Some recovered after many painful struggles, but two died; the one for which the prisoner now stands before you, and the other is

brood mare, belonging to Mr. Northey, and the circumstances which I shall prove, can leave no doubt
in any reasonable mind, as to the cause of death. I
shall prove to you that the horses were in sound
health, up to the 10th of July, and it is impossible to
draw any other conclusion than that they were poisoned. A skilful veterinary surgeon, who attended
the opening of the horse, will prove this fact, and a
skilful chemist, who analized the contents of a bottle,
will prove to you, that he found arsenic enough
about it to kill. Another important point for your
consideration is, did the prisoner infuse that poisonous liquid into the trough, because if he did, it im-
plies malice. I shall prove he was a frequenter of
Newmarket races, and a witness, who you will hear
to day, will state to you, that the prisoner arrived at
Newmarket, at the spring meeting, when a conversation took place betwixt the said witness and the prisoner, which I shall forbear to state, as you will
better judge of it from her own mouth. Dawson
lodged at her house, and she will prove his arrival at
Newmarket, two or three days before the July meeting. You will hear from her, that she discovered a
bottle concealed, in making Dawson's bed, and she
will best describe that event. On Saturday, the 8th

of July, previous to the commencement of the meeting on the 10th, the prisoner obtained of this witness,
two phials, and she will prove that he was from his
lodging at late hours on the nights of Saturday and
Sunday, when a candle was left burning for him at
his request, and his excuse was that he had gone to
see *Captain Barclay* walk his match. Dark deeds,
Gentlemen, are generally performed in the dark,
where the eye of observation can be baffled. This is
a natural cause, and it can only be got at by circumstances, which form a chain, but a concatenation of
evidence, which bind the links, cannot deceive, when
the positive testimony of one or two witnesses might,
by sinister motives. *Woodwellhead* had engagements
to perform, the first of which was on Monday, the
10th of July, and Mrs. Trumbull will relate to you
a particular conversation she had with Dawson, respecting this favourite horse. Close upon the time of
this horse attempting his first engagement, the prisoner offered to bett 20 to 1 against his winning,
and treated any notions of his chance of so doing
as nonsense. Dawson was at his lodgings when in-
telligence was brought to the house that some horses
were poisoned, and the conversation that passed on
such being known, will require particular attention.

After this event, the bottle I have before spoken of, vanished, and after the prisoner had left the same bottle, which would be identified, it was found empty, and concealed in a different part of the house. It was afterwards delivered to a gentleman of the name of *Weatherby*, at Newmarket, and on trying a test on the remnants, it will be proved by Mr. Fuller, a gentleman of consumate skill, and first practice, to have contained poison. These circumstances are cogent and strong, when coupled together, more so even than direct evidence. The prisoner made particular inquiries after this bottle on his return to Newmarket. If any doubt remain, the evidence of Bishop, the accomplice will remove it by his testimony; Such evidence is entitled to full credit as far as it is confirmed by other witnesses, and it will be found the most important, and there are no reasons to discredit it. He will prove to you that he prepared the solution for the prisoner with his own hand, and that he personally delivered it to him, and he will prove an acknowledgement from Dawson, that he had infused the poison in the trough, and killed a mare and hackney. I shall not occupy your attention further than to call it to two points; viz. whether ar' you satisfied the horse, the subject of this

indictment, died by poison, and whether you are satisfied the prisoner infused the poisonous liquid into the
water.

After the bustle in court, at the conclusion of the
council's speech had subsided, evidence was called
to prove the case, and to prove that the horses were
poisoned, the following witnesses were called:

Mr. Adams, of Royston, proved, that having left
his mare in the care of Mr. Stevens, a training groom,
at Newmarket. He went to the stables on Monday
morning, and found the animal down in the stall, in
apparent great agony, and she died on the same morning:

Cross examined by Mr. KING.

Q. Are you acquainted with the prisoner?

A. I knew him.

Q. Have you ever had any dispute with him?

A. No.

Re-examined by Mr. BEST.

Q. You knew him personally.

A. Yes, I saw him frequently.

Jones, an assistant groom to Mr. Stevens, in July,
1809, stated, that he had sixteen or seventeen in his
employ at different periods. Witness recollected

having Mr. Adams's hackney under his care in July, 1809, and he was in the habit of sending the horses under Mr. Stevens's care to water, and sometimes attended them. Mr. Adams's hackney was in good health on Sunday evening, the 9th, and was rode to water out of a trough, by Richard Clark, a boy. Witness saw the mare at five o'clock on Monday morning, the 10th, also before she went to the trough, and she was then in good health.

Question from the Judge.

Did she eat corn then?

A. Yes.

Witness saw the mare again, betwixt eight and nine o'clock on Monday morning, in the stable, when she was rolling about in great agony. She perspired a good deal, and had a kind of dizziness, and a violent purging. After continuing in this state about half-an-hour she died, and he afterwards saw her opened by a man named Clark. There were seven other horses in Mr. Stevens's stables, viz. two of Mr. Northey's, Mr. Adams's, Sir C. Banbury's *Agnes, Woodwellhead,* and *Fair Ellen,* they were all very violently effected, but they all recovered, excepting two. *Woodwellhead* was to run the following Wednesday.

Cross examined by Mr. KING.

How do you know *Woodwellhead* was about to run on the Wednesday?

A. I knew by the Calendar, as well as having had my orders of General Grosvenor.

Richard Clark, a boy, in the employ of Mr. Stevens, proved having rode Mr. Adams's mare to water on the morning of the 10th of July, 1809. She was very well before she watered.

Mr. Joseph Goodwin, a veterinary surgeon, who resided in London, but who lived at Newmarket in 1809, was called on to look at the horses in Mr. Stevens's stables, on the evening of the 10th of July. He saw the mare, the subject of this indictment, which was dead, before his arrival. The mare was opened under the inspection of witness, and there was a general inflammation round the intestines. Witness had opened horses which had died of a common inflammation, and in the present case, according to his experience, appearances were different. From the report which had spread respecting other horses, witness was induced to examine the body more particularly, and he found the stomach almost in a state of gangrene, and the cause of death appeared the same in both horses.

Question from one of the Counsel for the Prosecution.

What, according to your professional knowledge caused the death of Mr. Adams's mare?

A. From the circumstance of analysing the water, and arsenic having been found therein, I am of opinion, the mare died from the effects of poison.

Question from the Judge.

Did appearances indicate that the mare died of a natural inflammation, divesting yourself of what you heard relative to poisoning?

A. It certainly did not appear as a common case of inflammation.

Q. Have you known instances of common inflammation killing in a short time.

A. Such a thing is not unusual.

Question from Counsel.

You also opened Mr. Northey's mare.

A. Yes, and I attended the other horses sick.

Q. State your opinion upon the whole.

A. My opinion is, that one general cause produced the same effects on each horse, but I must be understood as speaking of the horses which did not die. Of those which died, the whole alimentary canal from the stomach to the intestines, produced appearances unlike those which appeared in common inflammations; but I never had occasion before to attend a horse which had been poisoned.

Q. Is it common for a horse which has a common inflammation to purge?

A. Not always, but it is not uncommon.

Cross-examined by Mr. King.

If it had not been for the report of a number of horses having been poisoned, what would have been your opinion as to the cause of inflammation.

A. I should not have made so minute an examination in one case alone, and it might have passed for a common inflammation.

Q. I understand you to state, that you never attended horses under similar circumstances.

A. No, I did not, but it struck me that there were something more in appearances than what is seen in common inflammations, and as I have before stated, from reports which were circulated, I should not probably have made so close an examination, but the inflammation had not the common appearances.

Thos. Payne, a servant, proved, having filled a bottle with water, which he took out of the trough where the horses had drank, and he delivered it to Lord Stawell.

Q. You are come here to speak the truth you know.

A. I should be sorry to tell a story.

Q. To whom did you first take this bottle, or mention that you found it, and at what time?

A. Why to Mr. Weatherly and Sir C. Bunbury. I don't know the time.

Q. Now listen Mrs. Trimbull.

A. Yes, and I will answer to, if I think proper.

Judge. You must answer, if you don't think proper.

Q. When did you tell Sir C. Bunbury, or Mr. Weatherly, I ask you again?

A. Why it was about the latter end of August, or the beginning of September.

Q. Did you ever mention about the bottle to any one else, and that Dawson had used you ill?

A. I might have given a hint that he had not used me well, because he was in my debt for rent.

Q. What, you harbour a grudge against him then?

A. No, I have no other grudge than he used me ill in not paying his rent; nobody would be pleased at that.

Q. Now, upon your oath, did not O'Mara tell

you, you would get some money for appearing here?

A. No, never.

Q. Upon the solemn oath you have taken, I ask, did he not tell you you would have some money coming after this trial, from some person?

A No, he never did say any such thing, nor did any one else.

Q. What, don't you know there were hand-bills posted about Newmarket, offering a reward for the discovery of this business?

A. I never saw any papers about it.

Q. Nor did you ever hear of a reward?

A. I might have heard such a thing, but one would have enough to do to listen to half what people say.

Q. You are very positive about the bottle you speak of, what marks are there on it, that you can swear so very exact about it?

A. Why there is a dent upon the shoulder of it.

Q. Then 'twas a lucky thing you happened to notice that dent.

A Yes, lucky enough.

Q. Was it such a bottle as you get at an apothecaries?

A. I don't know, I am sure.

Q. Perhaps you have no knowledge of what an apothecaries bottle is?

A. Have I not then, I ought to know, for I have had too many of them.

Mr. Edward Weatherby, race-manager, or keeper of the stud-book at Newmarket, stated, that Wood-wellhead had three engagements during the meeting, which commenced on Monday, July 10th, 1809. Witness proved, that Mr. Stevens's house was in the parish of Wood Ditton. He received the bottle of the last witness betwixt the July and October meetings, but could not tell the precise time. The bottle had a white sediment in the upper part of it, in the head or shoulder, although it seemed as if some pains had been taken to remove the remnants by washing it. Witness observed the bottle had a dent in it, which Mrs. Trimbull had pointed out, and it was afterwards delivered to Thomas Foy.

Q. I understand you to say, you can't call to your recollection the time you received the bottle of Mrs. Trimbull?

A. It was about the latter end of August, or the beginning of September.

Q. Was it subsequent to the inquiry and noise the business had occasioned?

A Yes, it was after the inquiry certainly.

Thomas Foy, an Officer of Marlborough-street police-officer, whose diligence and uuremitting exertions, brought both Dawson and Bishop to justice, after long and laborious pursuit, produced the bottle he had received of Mr. Weatherby, which had never been out of his sight, nor out of his possession excepting when Mr. Fuller tried his tests upon the sediment it contained.

Mrs. Tillbrook swore to the bottle being the same as she had found, when both full and empty.

Mr. Fuller was again examined, and he stated that he did not analize the substance, but examined it by test, so as to satisfy himself it contained arsenic. This gentleman entered into a scientific and learned statement in support of the conviction on his mind, that the bottle con ained poison, but after being examined, and re-examined by each side, one of the counsel said he was not *learned enough* to comprehend the statement of the witness, but that it was pretty generally understood in court. The Judge at length saved the counsel the trouble of making another such confession, by putting the following important question——" Is your judgment founded " upon a matter of opinion, or do you speak from

" a moral certainty?" Mr. Fuller answered—
" I speak as being morally certain. I know of no
" substance in nature, which would put on the same
" appearance.

Cecil Bishop, the accomplice of Dawson, whose
evidence was most important, stated, that he was
brought up a chemist and druggist, in the shop of
Mr. Baylis, Thayer-street, Manchester-square. Had
some slight knowledge of Dawson twelve months before; the latter knew witnesses situation, but they
became more acquainted when witness was at
Baylis's, in the spring of 1807. In 1808, witness
went to live at Mr. Gristock's, 66, Wardour-steeet,
and soon after the prisoner called on him,
and after purchasing some trivial article, he appeared rather surprised to see witness there. Dawson
stated that a friend of his had lost a match, by a trick
having been played off upon his horse, which was
taken suddenly ill. The prisoner desired to have
something which would produce the same effect.
Witness inquired whether the horse was young, as it
probably might be a cold, or a glandular affection.
Witness made up a bottle of *corrosive sublimate*, and
carried it to a public house, where he met the prisoner by appointment, and delivered it to him, in two
hours after it was ordered He called on witness

again, in three weeks after, and said he had tried the
effect on some dog horses, but it was not strong
enough. Witness made up a stronger bottle, and
delivered it to him, and the next time he saw him
was at Guy's hospital, where witness had a situation
as assistant apothecary. He went there in 1808, and
in the spring of 1809, Dawson called on him again,
and expressed the difficulty he had in finding him out,
and they went together and drank wine, in Jewin-
street, where Dawson said the stuff had not produced
the desired effect. The prisoner knew what the preparation was, witness having made him acquainted
with it in Soho-square, but he understood at that
time he wanted that which would prevent a horse
winning without materially injuring him. The prisoner said that was what he wanted, and witness next
prepared a solution of arsenic, which he took to
Dawson, at the King's Arms, in Holborn. This was
in the spring of 1809. He said the horses threw up
their heads when they smelt the former preparation,
and would not drink. The latter preparation was
made up in a pint bottle, and had no smell. Witness
told the prisoner to be careful how he used it, and
after understanding from Dawson, that the trough
into which he was about to infuse the solution, held

from ninety to one hundred gallons of water, he told him what quantity to put in, and he also gave him directions how to fill up the trough, as the horses drank out the water. If he went beyond these directions he would do away the effect of sickening, and kill the horses, for he had enough stuff to kill all the cattle at Newmarket, having been furnished with two other bottles at Bow-street, Bloomsbury. Dawson's reply was, " *Never mind that, they are all bl——y rogues at Newmarket, never mind killing, they would soon plunder you of a fortune at Newmarket, if you had one to loose, and they would not mind plundering me the same.*" The prisoner told witness he should not want £100 in case the thing answered. This was in the spring of 1809, and witness did not see the prisoner again, until the autumn, when the latter told him that he had put a double quantity of stuff into the trough, before it was filled up, and it turned out that a brood mare and a hackney had been poisoned. Witness wrote two or three letters for him, as he said there was a great piece of work about it, and suspicion had fell upon him. One of the letters was to Mr. Goodison, in vindication of Dawson's character.

Cross exrmined by Mr. KING.

You instruct well to make a rogue, Mr. Bishop, you are a very able master, where did you learn the art of poisoning horses so clearly?

A. I do not know.

Q. Where you ever in the army?

A. Yes, I was an ensign.

Q. On what account did you leave it?

A. Probably as many others leave the army, because I had no fortune to stay in it.

Q. Then I am to understand you left it voluntary?

A. No, I left it because I did not return in time—I was obliged to leave it.

Q. You have been at sea also, I believe.

A. No, I never was in the sea service.

Q. Pray what have you done for a living since you left the army?

A. I have been in the medical line.

Counsel. Yes, *that we understand.*

Q. From whence did you come now?

A. From confinement;—the custody of Mr. Bridge.

Q. I thought you had been at large?

A. No;—you took good care of that.

corroborative evidence. It was next to impossible in atrocious cases, to meet the ends of justice without this sort of evidence, as it seldom happened that eye witnesses could be found in these dark acts. A chain of circumstances combined was as strong as positive proof, as in that case persons may be suborned to swear falsely. As to the horse of Mr. Adams having been poisoned, no doubt could exist; then the next thing was for the jury to watch the conduct of the prisoner. He first cautions Mrs. Tillbrook against suffering her young woman to touch a bottle in his bed room. The circumstances of the woman finding the bottle concealed, the prisoner having been unusually late out on the two evenings, previously to the horses having been poisoned, were strong circumstances, if the witness was was to be believed, and her testimony had not been impeached: The prisoner has called no witnesses to prove where he was on those two evenings, which he might have done. The law of the case was decisive, even so as where death was occasioned in the act of procuring abortion, or any other murder. Mr. Fuller's testimony relative to the bottle which was found empty in Mrs. Tillbrook's house, proves from his vast knowledge and skill in his profession, that remnants of arsenic was in that bottle.

The Jury turned round in the box about four minutes, and returned a Verdict of GUILTY, *death*.

The Judge proceeded to pass sentence of death on the prisoner in the following words ;—

Daniel Dawson, after the patient investigation of your case, you have been convicted of an offence, which subjects you to a capital punishment. You had laid your atrocious plans with so much art and ingenuity, that you hoped to avoid detection, but the providence of God has at length overtaken you, and your wicked and barbarous acts have not remained undiscovered. The act of parliament upon which you have been convicted, was passed, to punish with death, those who should destroy the cattle of others, with intent to injure and impoverish, but you have been actuated by baser motives, your object was not merely to kill, but to win money by betting. After having been convicted of a crime so atrocious, let me admonish you to expect no mercy in this world: the dissolute life you have led ill prepares you for that awful tribunal, before which you must shortly appear to answer for your manifold crimes. Let me admonish you the short time you have to live, to make the best use of your time you can, allotted you in this world, in craving peace with God. It now remains with me to pass on you, the awful sentence of the law. You will be removed from this place to the place from whence you came, and from thence to a place of execution, where you will be hanged by the neck until you are dead, and the Lord in his infinite mercy receive your soul. The prisoner was conducted back to the Castle, in a post chaise, and is left for execution.

Bishop was ordered to be discharged, which was forthwith done.

DAWSON behaved with a sullen and impudent levity during the trial, and he frequently abused the witnesses whilst giving their testimony, loud enough to be heard throughout the court. Whilst the jury were considering their verdict, he was abusing Mrs. Trimbull, who stood near him, with horrid imprecations, ill becoming his unhappy situation, and at other times he was nodding at and saluting with his hand different persons in court. The verdict of GUILTY had not the slightest effect on him, and his general conduct was altogther depraved. On his return to the castle, his conduct, at times, bordered on insanity, and he appears too illiterate to feel a consciousness of wrong, although he has confessed his guilt to the full extent. He has not as yet given up any of his accomplices, but many are suspected, and probably ere this is at press, some important dis-coveries will have been made. Dawson states his disregard of death, and declares the only inconveni-ence he can feel in leaving this world, is parting from his wife, whom he represents as having been ill used by him, and for whom he has a desire only to live, to cherish and to atone for his misconduct. One of the most important witnesses on the case, named *Ellis*, has been got out of the way, and every attempt to find him failed.

The following letter was received from Brighton, on the 20th on the part of the prosecution.

" Brighton, July 18, 1812.

Sir,

I am sorry to inform you that Ellis is not to be found neither here nor at Newhaven, Seaford, or Lewes, he was here two nights and told Francis that he came fromSeaford where he had been with a horse, but I cannot find out any thing of any such horse, nor of any person at Seaford, that received any horse about that time, the only thing worth mentioning that I have heard or could make out, is, that when he was here, he was seen by Hicks's ostler often in Mr.

Brogrove's stable, and had some bets with Philip, Mr. B.'s man, and Donaldson, of the library, tells me, that he knows Ellis, and that he saw him and Brogrove conversing together on the Steyne, last Wednesday or Thursday morning.

I shall come to Cambridge on Tuesday morning.—I am inclined to think that Peek knows nothing of Ellis *this time*"

FINIS.

A few of the Pamphlets of the Trial of DAWSON at the Lent Assizes remain unsold, and can be had with the present one at the different Booksellers.

LONDON: PRINTED BY W. GLINDON, RUPERT-STREET, HAY-MARKET.

Lightning Source UK Ltd.
Milton Keynes UK
UKHW020759121222
413794UK00007B/554